WISE & WACKY WORKS
BY
Anonymous

RODNEY MARTIN • STEVEN WOOLMAN

For my parents.

(S.W.)

For Sandra.

(R.M.)

Produced by Martin International Pty Ltd
[A.C.N. 008 210 642] South Australia
Published in association with Era Publications,
220 Grange Road, Flinders Park, South Australia 5025

Text © Rodney Martin, 1993
Illustration © Steven Woolman, 1993
Designed by Steven Woolman
Printed in Hong Kong
First published 1993

National Library of Australia
Cataloguing-in-Publication Data:

Wise and wacky works by Anonymous.

Includes index.
ISBN 1 86374 039 2.
ISBN 1 86374 040 6 (pbk.).
ISBN 1 86374 041 4 (big bk.).

1. Poetry - Collections. 2. Children's poetry. 3. Humorous
poetry. I. Martin, R.D. (Rodney David), 1946-

808.81

Available in:
Australia from Era Publications, 220 Grange Road,
Flinders Park, South Australia 5025
Canada from Vanwell Publishing Ltd, 1 Northrup Cresc.,
PO Box 2131, Stn B, St Catharines, ONT L2M 6P5
New Zealand from Wheelers Bookclub, PO Box 35-586
Browns Bay, Auckland 10
Singapore, Malaysia & Brunei
from Publishers Marketing Services Pte Ltd, 10-C Jalan Ampas,
#07-01 Ho Seng Lee Flatted Warehouse, Singapore 1232
Southern Africa from Trade Winds Press (Pty) Ltd,
PO Box 20194, Durban North 4016 RSA
United Kingdom from Harcourt Brace Jovanovich Ltd, Foots Cray
High Street, Sidcup, Kent DA14 5HP (paperback & big book);
Ragged Bears Ltd, Ragged Appleshaw, Andover (hard cover)
United States of America from AUSTRALIAN PRESS ™,
c/- Ed-Tex, 15235 Brand Blvd, #A107, Mission Hills CA 91345

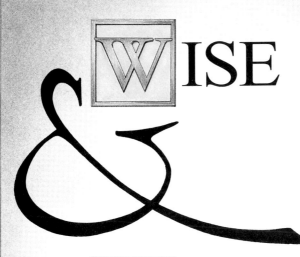

WISE

&

WACKY

WORKS

BY

Anonymous

Compiled and edited by Rodney Martin
Illustrated by Steven Woolman

CONTENTS

NTRODUCTION

Most people play with rhyme and verse at some time in their lives. Children chant verses while they play; adults recite verses to their children. In this way, verse is handed down from generation to generation, but the name of the author is often unknown or forgotten. The author is then listed as 'anonymous'.

Over the past ten years or so, I have visited many classrooms in various parts of the world and spoken with children and teachers about their best-loved verse. Often, we shared and compared traditional rhymes we knew — rhymes by anonymous authors.

Sometimes I overheard children chanting at play, or spied a verse in an autograph book I was signing, or was shown a variation of a verse I already knew. So my collection of wise and wacky verse by that unknown author, Anonymous, has grown over the years.

I hope that you enjoy the works of Anonymous in this book. By sharing them with others, you can play *your* part in keeping them alive for children and adults of the future.

Rodney Martin

CRAZY ANIMALS

THE GUINEA-PIG

There was a little guinea-pig,
Who, being little, was not big;
He always walked upon his feet,
And never fasted when he eat.
When from a place he ran away,
He never at that place did stay;
And while he ran, so I am told,
He ne'er stood still for young or old.
He often squealed (sometimes quite violent),
And when he squealed he ne'er was silent;
Though ne'er instructed by a cat,
He knew a mouse was not a rat.
One day, as I am certified,
He took a whim and fairly died;
And, so I'm told by those of sense,
He never has been living since.

Humans have always had a close association with the animals of the world. Anonymous saw the funny side of this, reminding us that perhaps animals and humans are not so different, as in *The cats of Kilkenny*; or giving us a tongue-in-cheek warning, as in *Algy and the bear*.

7

THE CORMORANT

The common cormorant, or shag,
Lays eggs inside a paper bag.
The reason you will see no doubt,
Is that it keeps the lightning out.
But what such unobservant birds
Have never noticed is that herds
Of wandering bears may come, with buns,
And steal the bags to hold the crumbs!

 THE CENTIPEDE AND THE FROG

A centipede was happy — quite,
Until a frog in fun
Said, "Which leg comes after which?"
This raised her mind to such a pitch,
She lay distracted in a ditch
Considering how to run.

THE CATS OF KILKENNY

There were once two cats of Kilkenny,
Each thought there was one cat too many;
So they fought and they fit,
And they scratched and they bit,
Till excepting their nails
And the tips of their tails,
Instead of two cats —
There weren't any!

I'VE GOT A DOG

I've got a dog as thin as a rail,
With fleas from his nose to the tip of his tail;
And every time his tail goes flop,
The fleas on the bottom all hop to the top.

ALGY AND THE BEAR

Algy met a bear,

A bear met Algy.

The bear was bulgy,

The bulge was Algy.

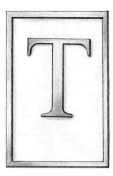

THAT'S LIFE

Anonymous often observed and commented on everyday aspects of life; sometimes showing us the ridiculous, as in *Peas and honey*; sometimes showing us wisdom, as in *The wise old owl*; but always making us smile.

CAPTAIN COOK

Captain Cook, he made some soup,
His mother made some jelly.
He forgot the soup was hot,
And burned inside his belly.

PEAS AND HONEY

I eat my peas with honey,
I've done it all my life.
It makes the peas taste funny,
But it keeps them on the knife.

THE WISE OLD OWL

The wise old owl sat in an oak,

The more he heard, the less he spoke;

The less he spoke, the more he heard.

Why aren't we all like that wise old bird?

FIVE LITTLE CHICKENS

Said the first little chicken,
With a quick little squirm,
"I wish I could find
A fat, little worm."

Said the second little chicken,
With an odd little shrug,
"I wish I could find
A fat, little slug."

Said the third little chicken,
With a sharp little squeal,
"I wish I could find
Some nice, yellow meal."

Said the fourth little chicken
With a small sigh of grief,
"I wish I could find
A juicy, green leaf."

Said the fifth little chicken,
With a faint little moan,
"I wish I could find
A tiny, smooth stone."

"Now, see here," said the mother,
From the green garden patch,
"If you want any breakfast,
You should come here and scratch."

JUST AND UNJUST

The rain it raineth every day,
Upon both just and unjust fella,
But more upon the just, because
The unjust hath the just's umbrella.

TO MIKE O'DAY

This is the grave of Mike O'Day,
Who died maintaining his right of way;
His right was clear, his will was strong,
But he's just as dead as if he'd been wrong.

PEOPLE ARE FUNNY

Anonymous often wrote about people's habits and even used their names in fun. However, Anonymous did exaggerate — just a little bit!

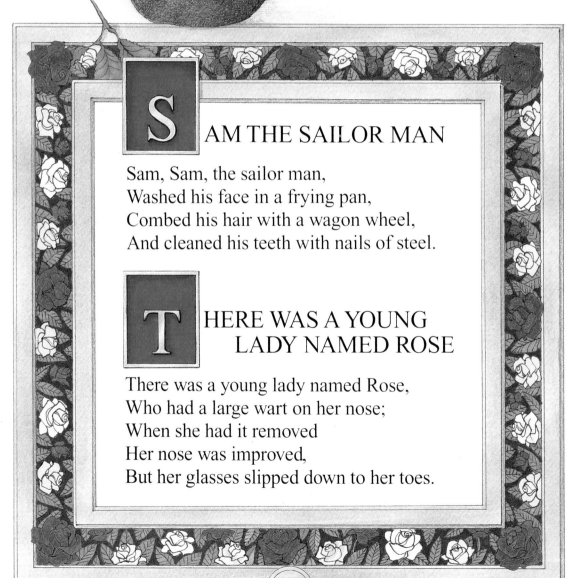

SAM THE SAILOR MAN

Sam, Sam, the sailor man,
Washed his face in a frying pan,
Combed his hair with a wagon wheel,
And cleaned his teeth with nails of steel.

THERE WAS A YOUNG LADY NAMED ROSE

There was a young lady named Rose,
Who had a large wart on her nose;
When she had it removed
Her nose was improved,
But her glasses slipped down to her toes.

PAPA MOSES

Papa Moses killed a skunk,
Mama Moses cooked the skunk,
Baby Moses *ate* that skunk.
My, oh my — oh how they stunk!

MY UNCLE LUKE

My Uncle Luke, he thinks he's cute, But Grandpa's even cuter.

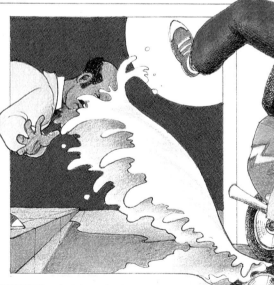

He's ninety-eight and stays out late, With Grandma on their scooter.

A STUDENT NAMED BESSOR

There once was a student named Bessor,
Whose knowledge grew lesser and lesser.
It at last grew so small,
He knew nothing at all,
So they made him a college professor.

MRS BROWN WENT TO TOWN

Mrs Brown went to town,
With her knickers hanging down.
Mrs Green saw the scene
And wrote it in her magazine.

Mrs Brown went to town,
To buy a can of peaches.
Mr Lees gave such a sneeze,
He blew the can to pieces.

OCTOR BELL

Doctor Bell fell down a well
And broke his collar-bone.
Doctors should attend the sick
And leave the well alone.

SISTER NELL

Into the family drinking well,
William pushed his sister Nell.
She's still there, because it kilt 'er —
Now we have to buy a filter.

YOU CAN'T BE SERIOUS!

Many of the wackiest works of Anonymous were based on impossible situations, ridiculous statements or contradictions. In fact, they were absolute nonsense!

THE FROG

What a wonderful bird the frog are.
When he sit, he stand almost;
When he hop, he fly almost.
He ain't got no sense hardly;
He ain't got no tail hardly either.
When he sit, he sit on what he ain't got
    — almost!

I HAD A LITTLE DONKEY

I had a little donkey,
And I fed him in a trough.
He grew so fat,
That his tail dropped off.
So I got me a hammer,
And I got me a nail,
And I made my little donkey
A brand new tail.

DAYS AND MONTHS

Thirty days hath September,
April, June and November.
All the rest have thirty-one,
Excepting February alone,
Which has twenty-four plus four
Till leap-year, when it has one more.

Thirty days hath September,
April, June and no wonder.
All the rest have sugar in their tea
Excepting Grandma,
Who rides a bike
Till the wheels fall off, then she goes on strike.

FATHER GOT THE WATER HOT

Father got the water hot,
Mother caught a flea.

She put it in the tea-pot
And made a cup of tea.

When Father put the milk in,
The flea came to the top.

When Mother put the sugar in,
The flea went POP!

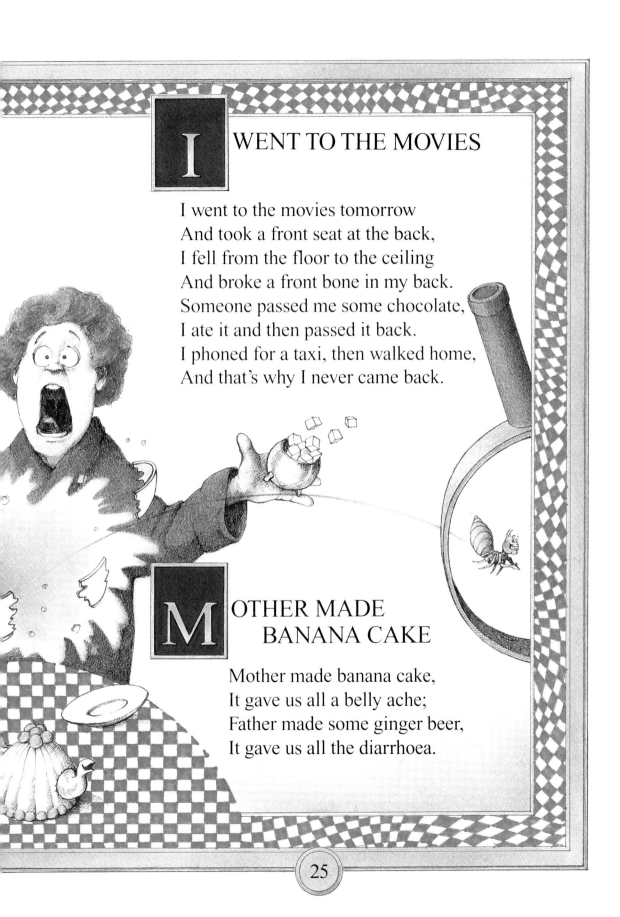

I WENT TO THE MOVIES

I went to the movies tomorrow
And took a front seat at the back,
I fell from the floor to the ceiling
And broke a front bone in my back.
Someone passed me some chocolate,
I ate it and then passed it back.
I phoned for a taxi, then walked home,
And that's why I never came back.

MOTHER MADE BANANA CAKE

Mother made banana cake,
It gave us all a belly ache;
Father made some ginger beer,
It gave us all the diarrhoea.

LAYING WITH WORDS

Anonymous often played with the sounds and meanings of words. Sometimes word sounds are used very cleverly, as in *The flea and the fly*; sometimes fun is made of the English language and its rules, as in *Shoeing the horse*; and sometimes words are changed for fun, as in *The sneeze*.

HETHER OR NOT

Whether the weather is fine
Or whether the weather is not,
Whether the weather is cold
Or whether the weather is hot,
We must weather the weather
Whatever the weather
Whether we like it or not!

MARY HAD A LITTLE LAMB

Mary had a little lamb,
His fleece was black as soot,
And everywhere that Mary went,
His sooty foot 'e put.

MARY ATE AN APRICOT

Mary ate an apricot,
Mary ate a plum,
Mary ran home
With a pain in her —
Now don't get excited
And don't be misled,
Mary went home
With a pain in her head.

27

HOEING THE HORSE

I said, "This horse, sir, will you shoe?"
And so, the horse, he shod.
I said, "This deed, sir, will you do?"
And so, the deed, he dod!
I said, "This stick, sir, will you break?"
And so, the stick, he broke.
I said, "This coat, sir, will you make?"
And so, the coat, he moke!

UZZY WUZZY

Fuzzy Wuzzy was a bear,

Fuzzy Wuzzy had no hair.

THE FLEA AND THE FLY

A flea and a fly in a flue,
Were trapped, so what could they do?
Said the fly, "Let us flee."
Said the flea, "Let us fly."
So they flew through a flaw in the flue.

So Fuzzy Wuzzy wasn't fuzzy — Was he?

THE TUTOR AND TOOTERS

A tutor who tooted her flute,
Tried to tutor two tooters to toot.
Said the two to the tutor,
"Is it harder to toot or
To tutor two tooters to toot?"

THE SNEEZE

I sneezed a sneeze into the air,
It fell to earth I know not where,
But hard and froze
Were the glares of those,
In whose direction I had snoze.

SAMUEL KNOTT

Here lies the body of Samuel Knott;
His father was Knott before him.
He lived Knott,
He died Knott,
And underneath this stone he lies,
Knott christened, Knott begot,
But most of all, forgot not.

NDEX BY TITLE